TRACK AND FIELD: Field Events

By Luke Thompson

HIGH interest books

Children's Press
A Division of Scholastic Inc.
New York / Toronto / London / Auckland / Sydney
Mexico City / New Delhi / Hong Kong
Danbury, Connecticut

Thanks to David Bowden and the girls' and boys' track and field teams of Boyd Anderson High School, Ft. Lauderdale, FL

Book Design: Victoria Johnson
Contributing Editors: Eric Fein and Matthew Pitt

Photo Credits: Cover and all photos by Maura Boruchow and Cindy Reiman except: p. 4 © Karl Weatherly/Corbis; p. 22 © Robert Maass/Corbis; pp. 23, 26 © Olivier Prevosto/Corbis; p. 24 © Neal Preston/Corbis; p. 29 © Duomo/Corbis; p. 38 © Jean-Ruszniewski/TempSport/Corbis

Visit Children's Press on the Internet at:
http://publishing.grolier.com

Library of Congress Cataloging-in-Publication Data

Thompson, Luke.
  Track and field: field events / Luke Thompson.
    p. cm. — (Sports clinic)
  Includes bibliographical references and index.
  ISBN 0-516-23169-3 (lib. bdg.) — ISBN 0-516-29565-9 (pbk.)
  1. Track-athletics—Juvenile literature. [1. Track and field.] I. Title. II. Series

GV1060.55 .T55 2001
796.43—dc21

2001017271

CONTENTS

INTRODUCTION

"Let's see who can throw this rock the farthest." For thousands of years, people have used phrases like this one. For thousands of years, people have also competed in one game or another. The ancient Greeks held the first Olympics more than two thousand years ago. Many of the running, jumping, and throwing events in the Olympic games of today are the same kind that were held in ancient Greece.

This book teaches the basics about field events. Field events can be divided into two types: jumping and throwing. There also are two combined events that mix jumping, throwing, and track into one competition.

Joining your track-and-field team can get you started in some of these events. You will be able to meet and compete against many different people. Track-and-field also is a great way to build your muscles and stay healthy. If you stay focused and practice hard enough, someday you might even win a gold medal.

For centuries, athletes have tested their physical skills in competitions.

5

ONE

FIELD EVENTS
TRAINING

Field events use all parts of your body. Therefore, your whole body needs to be in good physical condition. You want to develop a program that exercises your legs, arms, shoulders, stomach, back, and even your hands.

Stretching

Stretching and warming up your body before training or competition is important. Your legs, arms, and back are worked the hardest while doing field events. Most athletes warm up before and after they train and compete. The following stretches will help loosen your muscles and avoid injury. Repeat each stretch at least three times before going on to the next one.

Stretches such as this one keep your muscles loose.

Arms and Shoulders

Sit on the ground with your knees bent. Reach your hands back, keeping your palms flat. Lean back and flex your elbows as your shoulders rotate. When you feel your shoulder muscles stretch, stop and hold the stretch for 8 seconds.

Next, raise one arm above your head. Using the other arm, pull the raised arm (at the elbow) across the back of your head. Feel your muscles stretch along your arm and down your side. Hold the stretch for 8 seconds. Now stretch the other arm.

Stretching before a field event will reduce your risk of injury.

8

For this stretch to be effective, you must hold it for 8 seconds.

Legs and Back

Sit on the ground with your legs out in front of you. Slowly bend your back and touch your toes. Feel your back muscles stretch as you reach forward. Feel your calf and hamstring stretch as you touch your toes. Hold this stretch for 8 seconds.

Next, stand up with your legs close together. Bring one foot up behind your leg and hold it with your hand. Use a chair or the wall for support as you pull your heel against your body. Feel your thigh muscle stretch. Hold this stretch for 8 seconds, then stretch the other leg.

Training for field events works the muscles that are most used for these events. However, you want to work all your muscles to get your body into top physical condition.

You don't need to work out in a weight room to make your muscles strong. Push-ups, sit-ups, leg lifts, and other calisthenics work your muscles to help any sports training. If you add a pair of 6- or 8-pound hand weights to your workout, you can work your muscles into top shape without ever leaving home.

Sit-ups are an important part of any sports training program.

To get the best workout, do a series of each of the following exercises: ten sit-ups, ten push-ups, ten leg lifts, ten arm curls (with hand weights), and so on. Then repeat these series two times.

Did You Know?

Doctors believe that athletes should drink at least eight glasses of water every day. Water feeds muscles and helps them move quickly. Water also prevents muscle cramps and cleanses your body.

Eating the right foods keeps your body healthy. Fast foods and snacks are loaded with fat. Fat slows down your body and keeps your muscles from working well. A diet filled with fruits and vegetables gives your muscles power and speed. These foods also prevent sickness and disease.

The Food Pyramid

Dieticians study how healthful each type of food is. They suggest eating a variety of foods from each of the four food groups. The Food Guide Pyramid shows you which foods you should eat to stay healthy and strong. You should eat more foods from the bottom of the pyramid (breads and grains) than from the top (sugars and fats).

The Food Guide Pyramid offers suggestions for a healthy diet.

The Food Guide Pyramid

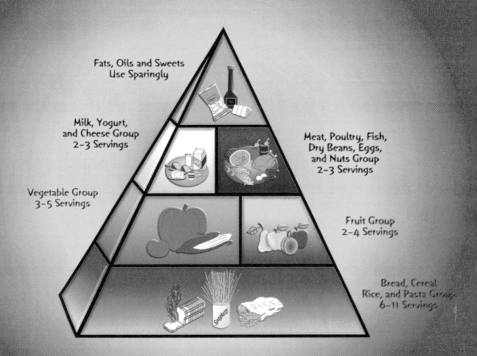

Fats, Oils and Sweets
Use Sparingly

Milk, Yogurt,
and Cheese Group
2–3 Servings

Meat, Poultry, Fish,
Dry Beans, Eggs,
and Nuts Group
2–3 Servings

Vegetable Group
3–5 Servings

Fruit Group
2–4 Servings

Bread, Cereal
Rice, and Pasta Group
6–11 Servings

A Guide to Daily Food Choices

TWO

JUMPING EVENTS

The long jump, the triple jump, the high jump, and the pole vault are the four jumping events held in a track-and-field competition.

The Long Jump

In the long jump, an athlete sprints down a runway toward a sandpit. The runway is 40 meters (m) long, or 131 feet (ft). The athlete jumps at the takeoff board and lands feetfirst in the sand. The length of the jump is measured from the end of the takeoff board to the first mark made in the sand. Each athlete gets six jumps. Judges record the athlete's best jump. There are four parts to the long jump: 1) the approach, 2) the takeoff, 3) the mid-air action, and 4) the landing.

The sandpit at the end of the runway helps this jumper make a soft landing.

5

Approach and Takeoff

Your approach run should be about fifteen running strides long. This is about how long it takes an athlete to reach his or her top speed. The last two strides set you up for the takeoff. You want to time your last foot plant to be on top of (but not beyond) the takeoff board. At the moment your foot hits the take-off board, jump. Your takeoff foot should be the foot that feels most comfortable jumping.

THE SHOES TO USE

Athletes can use spiked shoes for events that combine running and jumping. However, the shot put and discus (see chapter 3) require athletes to slide their feet or spin around. For these events, athletes wear regular sneakers or shoes with leather soles.

Jumping Events

Mid-Air Action and Landing

There are two mid-air actions that set up long jumpers for the landing. The first is the hang technique. For the hang, bring your legs together and out in front of you as you jump. The hang gets you quickly into the landing stance.

The hitch-kick technique is like running in the air. When you jump, keep your legs moving as if you were still running. Just before landing, stretch your legs out.

This long jumper uses the hang technique to prepare for landing.

Jumpers who use the hitch-kick technique look like they're running in the air

No matter which of the two techniques you use, you want to hit the sand with your legs stretched out in front of your body. You should have enough force carrying you forward so that you do not fall backward. Most jumpers hit the sand and bounce forward.

Jumping Events

The triple jump is a hop, step, and jump into the sandpit. Each of these movements gives you a takeoff spot that helps you gain distance. The triple jump uses the same track as the long jump, but the takeoff board is farther away from the sandpit. The shorter takeoff point gives you room to complete the hop, step, and jump and land in the sandpit. Each athlete gets six jumps. The best jump is recorded by the judges.

Figure 1

Each takeoff is done on a single leg, alternating for each takeoff. You don't want to put all your effort into one long jump. That's not the idea here. You want to increase your distance with each jump.

At the instant the triple jumper hits the takeoff point, he begins the hop from his strong leg.

When you hit the takeoff point, hop from your strong leg (Figure 1). The hop springs you forward as far as possible without disrupting your speed or body control. You land on your weak foot and immediately jump again. This is the step. The step transfers you from your weak foot back to your strong foot. The step is the shortest of the three jumps. You are rebounding from the force of the hop. At the same time, you are loading up for the jump (Figure 2). The step should be an easy gliding motion. As with the hop, you want to maintain as much of your original speed as possible.

Figure 2

The jumper has landed on his weak foot and completed the step. Now back on his strong foot, he loads up for the final jump.

Jumping Events

The jump is the final push for your overall distance. The jump carries you into the sandpit. As you land on your strong leg, jump up and swing up your weak leg. This brings both legs together and puts you in your landing position (Figure 3). Land with both feet in the sand with your weight moving forward.

It takes a lot of practice to find your comfort zone in the triple jump. You have to get a feel for how best to keep moving forward from one jump to the next.

Figure 3

As he heads for the sandpit, the jumper swings his weak leg up with his strong leg. He is now in perfect landing position.

The High Jump

In the high jump, athletes leap over a lightweight bar set on two posts. Athletes get three tries at leaping each height. The bar slowly is raised until only one athlete remains who can clear it. There are two steps to every successful high jump: the run-up and the jump.

In the high jump, run-ups are performed at an angle.

The Run-Up

The run-up is the approach an athlete takes to the bar. The run-up zone is no less than 30 m (98 ft) from the bar. A high jumper always approaches the bar from the opposite side of his or her jumping leg (strong leg). The high jump run-up is not a straight run at the bar. High jumpers run up to the bar at an angle. An angled jump gives a high jumper the most time and distance to get into the air and over the bar.

The Jump

To succeed at the high jump, you need to decide which foot you will be jumping from. As you sprint toward the jump zone, you begin to turn in. When you reach the takeoff point, your body should be nearly sideways to the bar.

At the takeoff, you drive yourself upward by lifting the knee of your leading leg as high as possible.

Your back foot pushes you off the ground. This action forces your body to twist away from the bar. As your body goes over the bar, it bends into an arc shape. The last thing you do is pull your legs over the bar as your body completes its arc.

During the takeoff, high jumpers push off with their back foot.

The Fosbury Flop

High jumpers use the Fosbury Flop to jump the bar. This technique was designed by athlete Dick Fosbury to use all of the body's flexibility. Fosbury used this method to win the high jump during the 1968 Olympics. Before the Fosbury Flop, high jumpers tried to go over the bar face down. Fosbury discovered that the body does not make a smooth arc while it is face down. The Fosbury Flop is performed face up, with the jumper's back to the ground.

This high jumper leaps over the bar face up. This technique is known as the Fosbury Flop.

Jumping Events

The Pole Vault

In the pole vault, athletes use a flexible pole to help them vault over a bar high off the ground. As in the high jump, athletes get three tries at each height. The athlete who clears the greatest height wins the competition. There are five stages to pole vaulting: 1) the approach, 2) the plant, 3) the takeoff, 4) the ride, and 5) the clearance.

POLE LENGTH

Poles can be any length. They tend to be about 14 feet (4m) long. Vaulters use poles that are shorter than the height of the bar they are jumping over. A shorter pole gives vaulters room in the air to turn their bodies and push themselves over the bar. A pole that is longer than the height of the bar will hit the bar and knock it down.

During the plant, the pole is brought down into a box.
When the pole catches in this box, it flexes.

The Approach

The approach is the sprint down a 40 m (131 ft) track carrying the pole. You hold the pole with both hands. Your strong hand should be at the top of the pole. Hold the pole at an upward angle as you run down the track.

The Plant and Takeoff

As you near the end of the runway, bring the pole down into a box. This action is called the plant.

Jumping Events

The box is a hole in the ground that catches the end of the pole. When the pole catches, it flexes. As the pole flexes and your body moves forward, you begin to go up into the air (see photo at left). Now you begin your takeoff.

At the takeoff, jump up with all your strength. As you jump, pull with your arms and let your legs swing forward. The combination of the flexing pole, your speed, and your final jump vaults you up into the air. The pole is completely flexed and your back is pointed to the ground. Your legs are in the air and you are letting the pole rebound from its flex. Now you are riding the bar.

The Ride

The ride is the action your body takes while in the air. Your body rocks back and its weight produces more action in the pole. The flexing pole carries your weight and bends. As the pole unbends, you move upward in the ride stage. Your feet now rise over your body. At the top of the ride, the pole unbends and your feet point straight up. This helps push you up and over the bar.

The Clearance

The final stage of the vault is clearing the bar. Your feet are the first to go over. Your arms still are holding the pole tightly. Now is the time to give a last push and let go. As you push off the pole, your body arcs over the bar and you fall onto the padded landing mat.

Jumping Drill: Heading a Suspended Ball

This exercise will improve both your leg strength and your ability to jump high. Get a lightweight ball the size of a soccer ball and a length of rope. Tie one end of the rope tightly around the ball. The other end of the rope should be tied to a strong tree limb or basketball net. Practice a running jump that lets you hit the ball with your forehead. As your jumping gets stronger, raise the ball higher.

In this pole vaulter's clearance, her feet are the first to go over the bar.

28

THREE

THROWING
EVENTS

There are four throwing events in the field competition: the shot put, the discus, the javelin, and the
hammer. This book focuses on the first three
events. A different object is thrown for each event.
How each object is thrown depends on its shape
and weight.

Shot Put

In the shot put, athletes compete against
one another by tossing shots. A shot is a
heavy ball about the size of a softball.
Shots can weigh anywhere from 1 lb (.5 kg)
to 16 lb (7.25 kg). The heaviest shots are
used in national, international, and Olympic
competitions. The athletes stand inside a 6-
foot-diameter circle and toss the shot out into a

A shot is about the size of a softball, but weighs a lot more.

marked landing zone. Competitors cannot go beyond the stop board (curved piece of wood at the front edge of the circle). Each athlete gets six tosses. The best toss is recorded.

The glide technique is the easiest way to put a shot. The idea is to position your body like a spring, and then let it loose. You start at the back of the ring, your back to the stop board. Hold the shot in the palm of your throwing hand below your chin. The shot should touch or be close to your

Here, the shot put thrower performs the glide technique. He begins with the shot at his chin (Figure 1). Then he bends his body down (Figure 2).

Figure 1

Figure 2

chin (Figure 1). The shot cannot be held below your shoulders. Bend your upper body toward the ground and act like a spring (Figure 2). Now slide your feet steadily to the middle of the ring and then, all at once, spring into motion (Figure 3). Your legs should spring first, then your hips and upper body. When your body springs up and out, push your arm out with all its strength and release the shot (Figure 4). Make sure your body does not go beyond the stop board.

Springing into motion, he slides his feet forward (Figure 3). As he takes his final step, the shot is released (Figure 4).

Figure 3

Figure 4

The discus is a plate-shaped object that spins through the air when thrown. Athletes throw the discus from a circle almost 8 feet (2 m) in diameter. They cannot go beyond the white lines of the circle. The discus flies out into a landing area and must fall within that area. Each athlete gets six throws. Again, the best one is recorded.

The rotary technique is the only way to throw a discus for great distance. The idea is to rotate (spin) the body around as fast as possible and then let go of the discus at the right moment. Most athletes will rotate three times before throwing.

The discus is shaped like a plate. An athlete gets six attempts to throw it as far down the field as possible.

Centrifugal Force

Centrifugal force is a term used by physicists. It explains how force increases quickly as an object moves away from the center of its rotation. Spinning your body while holding the discus increases the force and speed of the discus when you throw it.

Figure 1

Figure 2

The discus thrower begins with his back to the landing area (Figure 1). He then starts spinning forward inside the circled area (Figure 2).

Start at the back of the circle with your back to the landing area (Figure 1). Hold the discus with the flat side against your palm. Let the discus rest on the tips of your four fingers. Then let your arm hang down at your side. Wind your body back and begin spinning forward (Figure 2). It is important for you to spin on the balls of your feet and move toward the front of the circle. Spin three times, gaining speed with each spin (Figure 3). As your body comes around the last time, plant your front foot, swing your arm around, and throw the discus up and out (Figure 4). The rest of your body will continue to whip around. Timing the release of the discus is the key to a good throw.

Figure 3

Figure 4

At the end of the third spin, the thrower plants his front foot (Figure 3). He finishes by whipping his arm around and releasing the discus (Figure 4).

The javelin is a spear-shaped object that is between 6 and 7 feet (1.8–2.1 m) long. It is thrown from behind a line and must fall within a marked area. Competitors get six throws each.

A good javelin throw will send the javelin flying in a high arc with little or no wobble. Wobbling slows down the javelin and shortens its distance. When throwing the javelin, you want to

This athlete shows good form on her javelin throw. She is in a perfect spot to snap the javelin forward.

approach the foul line with as much speed as possible. The body's job is to take this speed and transfer it into a strong throw.

The runway to the foul line is 115 ft (35 m) long. Hold the javelin up and behind your back. Take long strides as you run toward the foul line. When you reach the foul line, plant the leg that is opposite from the side that is holding the javelin. Bring your body and arm forward. Snap your arm forward and release the javelin into the air (see photo at left). The idea is to throw the javelin like you're cracking a whip.

Throwing Drill: Practicing the Rotary Style

This drill will help you get more power into your discus throws. Draw a large circle on the ground. Use a lightweight rubber ring for your throws. First start with just one rotation. As you get better with your timing and release, increase the speed and number of your rotations. Aim for the same spot every time.

COMBINED EVENTS: THE HEPTATHLON AND DECATHLON

If you are an athlete who competes well at running, jumping, and throwing events, then you ought to try the combined events. Women compete in the seven-event heptathlon. Men compete in the ten-event decathlon. Competition takes place over two days. These multi-sport events are designed to test your all-around ability. Points are awarded based on how well you finish in each event. A first-place finish earns you many more points than fifth or last place.

Most combined-events athletes are stronger at some events than others. The idea is to train equally for each event. Your point total will be greater than if you focused only on those events in which you excel.

THE HEPTATHLON (women only)
The seven events are run in this order:
100-meter (328 ft) hurdles
Shot put
High jump
200-meter (656 ft) sprint
Long jump
Javelin
800-meter (2,625 ft) run

THE DECATHLON (men only)
The ten events are run in this order:
100-meter (328 ft) sprint
Long jump
Shot put
High jump
400-meter (1,312 ft) run
110-meter (361 ft) hurdles
Discus
Pole vault
Javelin
1500-meter (4,921 ft) run

NEW WORDS

calisthenics body exercises

centrifugal force the force that increases an
object's speed as it spins outward from
a middle point

decathlon a men's combined event of ten track
and field events

flex to bend

Fosbury Flop a style of high jumping where the
athlete jumps over the bar face up

glide technique a style of shot-putting that uses
only half a rotation

hang technique a long jump technique where
the feet are held together in the air

heptathlon a women's combined event of seven track-and-field events

hitch-kick technique a long jump technique in which the legs continue to run after the jump

leading leg in jumping events, this is the free leg that is not making the jump

rotate to turn

rotary technique a way to throw a discus by spinning around before releasing the discus

FOR FURTHER READING

Jackson, Colin and Gwen Torrrence. *The Young Track and Field Athlete.* New York: DK Publishing, Inc., 1996.

Wright, Gary. *Track and Field: A Step-by-Step Guide.* Mahwah, NJ: Troll Communications L.L.C., 1990.

Organizations

Track-and-field camps are located all over the United States. Your high school or local college might have one. The U.S.A. Track & Field organization lists dozens of youth camps across the country. Contact them to locate a camp in your area.

U.S.A. Track & Field
1 RCA Dome, Suite 140
Indianapolis, IN 46225
www.usatf.org/youth

Web Sites

Track & Field News

www.trackandfieldnews.com

Learn about your favorite field stars at this site. Find competition results and search the record books. There also are listings of United States high school All-American teams.

American Track & Field

www.runningnetwork.com/atf

Use this site to find running events in your area. Learn training and competition tips from the pros. Find out what's happening in the world of running.

United States Olympic Committee

www.usoc.org

Learn about all the Olympic sports, including track and field. Search for profiles of your favorite athletes. This site also has a museum that provides information about Olympic history.

INDEX

C
calisthenics, 10
centrifugal force, 36

D
diet, 12
discus, 31, 35, 37, 39

F
flex, 8
Food Guide Pyramid, 12

G
glide technique, 32

H
hang technique, 17
high jump, 15, 22–23
hitch-kick technique, 17

J
javelin, 31, 38–39
jump zone, 23

L
long jump, 15

M
muscle, 7–10, 12

O
Olympics, 5

P
pole vault, 15, 25

R
rotary technique, 35
run-up, 22

About the Author

Luke Thompson was born in Delaware. He holds a degree in English literature from James Madison University. He currently lives in Vail, Colorado.